PAELLA AND CHIPS

JIM HUTCHINGS

 Robson Books

First published in Great Britain in 1988 by Robson Books Ltd,
Bolsover House, 5–6 Clipstone Street, London W1P 7EB.

Copyright © 1988 Jim Hutchings

British Library Cataloguing in Publication Data

Hutchings, Jim
  Paella and chips : a cartoon guide to
  package holidays.
  I. Title
  741.5'942

ISBN 0-86051-544-3

Printed in Great Britain by
Billing & Sons Ltd., Worcester

Good grief woman do you really need this many
brochures?

One thing's for certain, we're not going to an hotel
where there's a happy hour four times a week, I
had enough of you last year!

Spain again? 'Course it's flippin' Spain again, they never think I might want to see the Blackpool illuminations!

Pick one and let's get to bed!

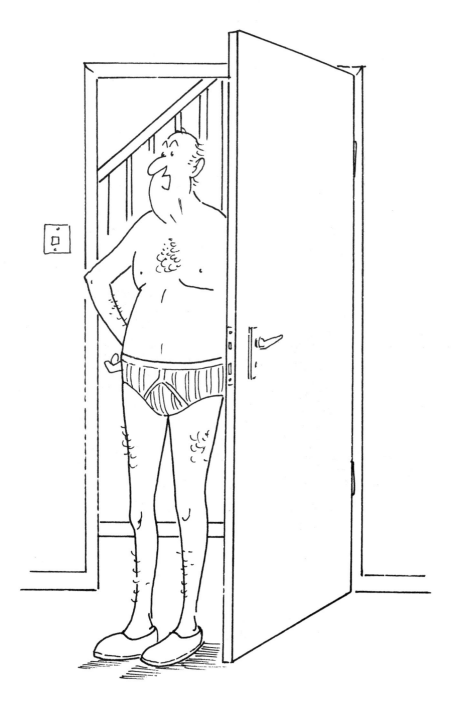

Every blasted year's the same, you're packing *too damned early!*

It's thanks to *you* remember, we can't go back to
Majorca again this year!

That's me packed—now what are you taking?

Oh hell, I know what this means, Spain again for
them and two weeks in the bloody cattery for me!

So where's *my* last minute crushable packing then?

Why get so depressed about it? Look on the
occasion as a fine opportunity to cement new
relationships, perhaps mix with others less fortunate
than yourself, and apart from that you selfish bitch
we need the holiday!

Do hurry dear the taxi's waiting.

Not that bloody check-list *again* Phyllis?

Hurry Maurice the cases are just going on the roof-
rack—focus on the labels for the destination and
hotel!

When we see our flight disappearing through the clouds, just remember it was *me* who wanted to take the scenic route to Gatwick.

Of course I can manage the camera dear, why
d'you ask?

I have to let him take it. He gets bored just sitting about on the beach.

Eight hours we've been here 'cause he got confused
with the twenty-four hour clock!

Camping? No we're not camping. He brings that
lot in case there's a flight delay.

Not *you* Doris—get off!

If we didn't need a holiday before, we'll bloody
well need one by the time we get to this gate
number!

Would you take your seats and *then* argue who did
or didn't cancel the newspapers and milk.

Our first flight is it madam?

Do you think the pilot would mind just popping back to Gatwick, my husband thinks he's left the car lights on.

It says here dear, 'Should you experience air pressure changes in the ears during climb or descent, you should yawn a few times.'

I knew they crowded you in on these charter flights,
but I didn't know it was this bad.

I should point out to those booked into the Hotel Splendido that the picture in our brochure *was* an artist's impression.

No. *We're double* booked your lot must be triple
booked!

D'you remember saying, 'To hell with paying extra
for a sea view?'

Hang on with that Edna—let's get unpacked first!

They're right enough dear, you *can* see the sea from
this balcony.

Where shall I put this then?

Well, now I see it on Maud it does seem a bit glitzy
for you.

Strewth Ethel the things you pack.

You're always the same, you take no damned
interest in the packing then never stop moaning
about what I haven't packed for you!

You and your blasted phrase book. Why don't you
point to the key or ask for it in English?

Emotee? No comprendo emotee senor!

Well I can never get a bloody *sunbed!*

It's no good getting depressed and disenchanted
with the Mediteranean Muriel, in any sea or ocean
in the world you're likely to see a condom.

A fat lot that damned rep knows telling us to
haggle with the local traders!

Oh my God Gladys, here comes that couple who've
been here twice before.

Well just a towel is enough for everyone else to
reserve a sunbed.

By God Molly, I do miss our ol' double bed back
'ome don't you?

Take a card to Viv and Ken. Arrived Palma Sunday
twenty first inst—

Good God Beryl, two days ago you'd never been
topless, now I think you'd be happy with a drum
roll!

Well Gerald, you're *never* going to join in the
birdie song if you don't keep practising.

I wish you'd *buy* some blasted castanets and leave
my dentures alone!

No, he's nobody famous dear, he just burns easily.

Damn it Vera, am I to spend the whole fortnight in
the doghouse just because I forgot to programme
the video to tape EastEnders?

Where do you want to sit then?

You *do* look daft with that, why don't you pay for
a hotel security box?

Of course he's not looking for trouble Rachel, put
him down.

This holiday's the wife's choice. Next year we'll
probably go where she wants to go.

Trust you to want the bottom one!

—and don't get any ideas about *me* going topless!

It seems someone's got hold of *today's* newspaper
dear.

Try it, you'll feel so liberated and free.

I wouldn't have come back here myself but my wife
Sybil fancies the wine waiter.

Warm the pot young man, and if you must use
teabags use one for each person, then take the
teapot to the hot water not the other way about,
and make sure the water's boiling, stir it, then leave
it to brew—

Did you see him jump to it when I said Judith
Chalmers and Cliff Mitchelmore?

I've had a word with the manager dear, and it
definitely *shouldn't* have been in the paella.

My mum doesn't like this buffet self service, but
I'm not complaining!

Don't be rude dear, perhaps his colloquial English
doesn't extend to 'bugger off' and 'sling your hook.'

He's a bit fed up. He's met a couple in the hotel
who paid a hundred pounds less than we did.

Y'now Fred, you could almost imagine you were in
Skeggy.

We like to bring the kids abroad, broadens their minds y'know.

You swine Cyril. You told me they couldn't get you
on that thing!

The travellers cheques Eric, throw down the
travellers cheques!

It's all right dear, it's not civil war breaking out,
it's the barbeque excursion getting back!

You'll love the freedom of self catering she said!

Why don't you try one out at a time then, till you
get used to the idea.

She's gone into town to do a spot of Christmas gift shopping and the fact that it's July has nothing to do with anything.

I suppose tonight they'll all be telling us what we missed by not going on the excursion today.

Those crazy Inglés, chef! They *actually* ate it!

'Cuatorcientos veinticinco pesetas por favor senor.'
'How much did he say again dear?'

Twenty-nine cards you've written and you have to
ask *me* what to write to your mother!

Well you can't go topless *and* be shy about it
Daphne!

Of course I know there're gadgets and sprays for
midges but they're not half as much fun.

God, I'm bored.

Hurry Doris, the maids are at the far end. If we
leave now we won't have to tip 'em.

I told you this would happen if you kept on feeding
those blasted cats!

Uno momento senora.

I *told* you to fix that case Gerald, I swear that's a
pair of your 'Y' fronts coming round.

Steady on Cynthia, you're looking just like four
litres over the limit.

A four-hour flight delay at Malaga, directed to
Luton from Gatwick, we get stopped by customs,
the Luton to Gatwick transfer coach breaks down,
I've still got jippy tummy, so tell me then what the
hell else could possibly happen?

Damn it Fiona, you must have some idea where I
left it!

Make up your mind dear, this morning you were
complaining about the stinking heat in Palma!

—and remember—the fact that it rained for five
days out of the fourteen is none of their damn
business!

George complained about the quality of the hotel
toilet paper, but apart from that it was lovely.

The holiday dear? No, no one's asked me a word
about it yet!

Don't go boring them with our holiday photos,
unless of course they bore us with theirs.